Rookie
Biography

ALEXANDER HAMILTON

American Hero

by K.C. Kelley

Content Consultant

Nanci R. Vargus, Ed.D.
Professor Emeritus, University of Indianapolis

Reading Consultant

Jeanne M. Clidas, Ph.D.
Reading Specialist

Children's Press®
An Imprint of Scholastic Inc.

Library of Congress Cataloging-in-Publication Data
Names: Kelley, K. C., author.
Title: Alexander Hamilton: american hero/By K.C. Kelley.
Description: New York, NY : Children's Press, an Imprint of Scholastic Inc.,
2017. | Includes index.
Identifiers: LCCN 2016030344| ISBN 9780531222904 (library binding)
| ISBN 9780531227718 (pbk.)
Subjects: LCSH: Hamilton, Alexander, 1757-1804—Juvenile literature. |
Statesmen—United States—Biography—Juvenile literature. | United States—Politics and
government—1783-1809—Juvenile literature.
Classification: LCC E302.6.H2 K454 2017 | DDC 973.4092 [B]—dc23
LC record available at https://lccn.loc.gov/2016030344

Produced by Spooky Cheetah Press
Design by Judith Christ-Lafond
Poem by Jodie Shepherd

Printed in China 62

SCHOLASTIC, CHILDREN'S PRESS, ROOKIE BIOGRAPHIES™, and associated logos are trademarks and/ or registered trademarks of Scholastic Inc.

1 2 3 4 5 6 7 8 9 10 R 26 25 24 23 22 21 20 19 18 17

Photographs ©: cover main: Alexander Hamilton, c.1804 (oil on canvas), Trumbull, John (1756-1843)/© Collection of the New-York Historical Society, USA/Bridgeman Art Library; cover inset: Joseph J Chakkungal/Shutterstock, Inc.; cover background, back cover background: STILLFX/Thinkstock; 3: Rudy Balasko/Shutterstock, Inc.; 4: Thomas Hamilton Crawford/Science Source; 8-9: Encyclopaedia Britannica/ UIG/Getty Images; 10-11: The Battle of Cowpens 1781 Daniel Morgan's, 1996 (w/c & gouache on paper), Troiani, Don (b.1949)/Private Collection/Bridgeman Art Library; 12: Everett Collection/ Superstock, Inc.; 13: Ralph Earl/The Granger Collection; 14: Frank Paul/Alamy Images; 15: Ed Vebell/ Getty Images; 16: North Wind Picture Archives/The Image Works; 18-19: DeAgostini/Superstock, Inc.; 20: Ed Vebell/Getty Images; 21: sinopics/iStockphoto; 22: imageBROKER/Superstock, Inc.; 23: Archive Photos/Getty Images; 24-25: Lee Snider/Alamy Images; 27: Sarin Images/The Granger Collection; 29: Nancy Carter/North Wind Picture Archives; 30: Pgiam/Getty Images; 31 top: Jim McMahon; 31 center top: North Wind Picture Archives/The Image Works; 31 center bottom: Sarin Images/The Granger Collection; 31 bottom: Ed Vebell/Getty Images; 32: Pgiam/Getty Images.

Maps by Mapping Specialists.

TABLE OF CONTENTS

Meet Alexander Hamilton

Alexander Hamilton is one of America's Founding Fathers. He grew up poor but was **determined** to change his life. With hard work, he made his dreams come true. Alexander Hamilton fought to make America free. And his ideas helped make the new country strong.

Alexander Hamilton was born on January 11, 1755, on the island of Nevis in the West Indies. He did not grow up with his father. The family was very poor. When Hamilton was 11, he got a job as a clerk. Then, when he was just 13, his mother died. He had to take care of himself.

FAST FACT!

When Hamilton lived in Nevis, it was a part of Great Britain.

NEW YORK

New York City ■

Area enlarged

UNITED STATES

WEST INDIES

Nevis ○

MAP KEY

○ Island where Alexander Hamilton was born

■ City where Alexander Hamilton lived

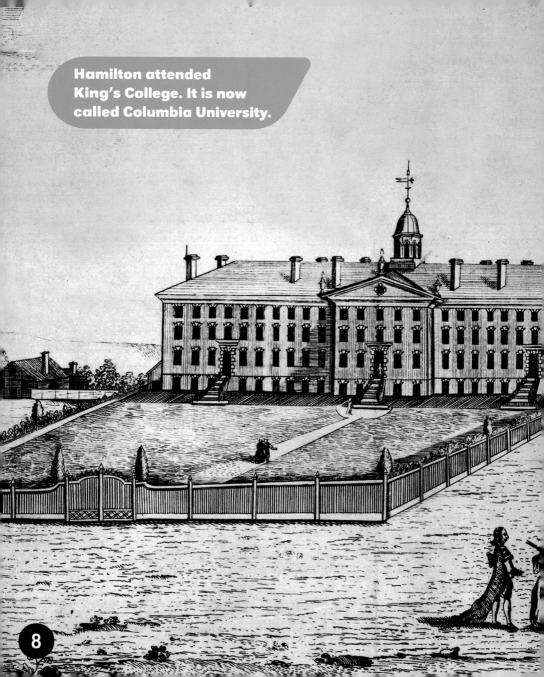

Hamilton attended King's College. It is now called Columbia University.

Hamilton was very smart. And he was a hard worker. His boss knew he had a lot of promise. He helped pay for Hamilton to go to college in New York City. America was a British **colony**. It was ruled by the king of England. Many Americans wanted to be free of England. Hamilton was one of them.

Hamilton the Soldier

Hamilton was a very good writer. In college, he wrote about America's fight for freedom. In 1775, the Revolutionary War began. The Americans formed an army to fight the British. Hamilton joined the army. He fought to help America be free.

The Americans fought many battles against the British.

George Washington leads his troops at Valley Forge, Pennsylvania.

George Washington was the leader of the American troops when Hamilton joined the army. He noticed Hamilton's writing skills and made him his assistant. Hamilton helped him plan battles.

While working for the general, Hamilton met Elizabeth Schuyler (right). He married her in 1780. They had eight children together.

In 1781, American and British forces fought the Battle of Yorktown. Hamilton led a charge on the enemy.
The Americans won that battle and the Revolutionary War. Hamilton had helped make America free!

Hamilton's first job in the army put him in charge of cannons. He showed his men how to point and fire them.

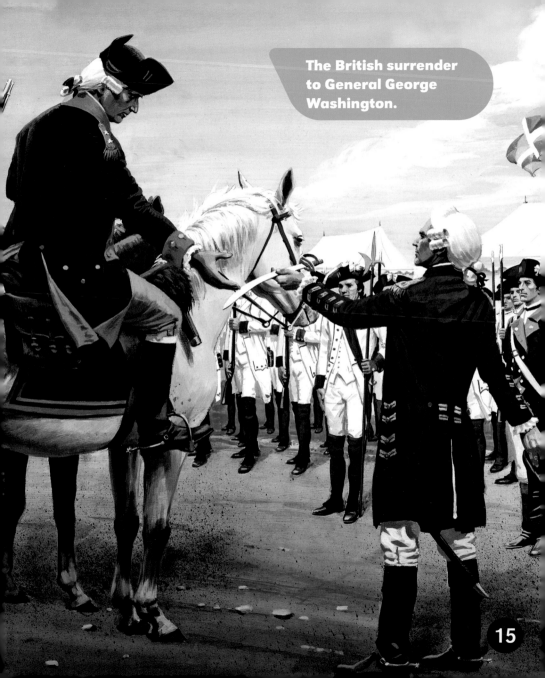

The British surrender to General George Washington.

Hamilton's work helped create some of the basic laws of the new nation.

Hamilton

Building a Nation

After the war, Hamilton became a lawyer in New York. Lawyers help people solve problems. Hamilton was one of the best. He even helped people who had different beliefs than he did.

Some people in New York had not supported the Revolution. Hamilton helped them anyway.

In 1787, American leaders met to plan the new Constitution. This was a document that would set up how the United States would be run. Hamilton wrote articles that called for a strong government. His ideas helped shape the Constitution.

American leaders meet at the Constitutional Convention in 1787.

President Washington asks Hamilton to be secretary of the Treasury.

President Washington asks Hamilton to be secretary of the Treasury.

The Constitution was approved in 1789. That year, Washington became the first president of the United States. He made his former assistant secretary of the **Treasury**.

Hamilton was pictured on this postage stamp in 1957.

Hamilton created a way to help the government keep track of its money. This helped America start off strong. He also set up the U.S. Mint. The Mint prints money and makes coins.

Hamilton's face is on the front of the U.S. $10 bill.

The first Mint in America was built in Philadelphia in 1792.

23

In 1802, Hamilton built the Grange, a large home in New York City. Today, it is open to the public.

Good Life, Sudden Death

In 1795, Hamilton left the government. He went back to being a lawyer. He and Elizabeth raised their family together. But their happiness would end suddenly. Hamilton had an enemy. His name was Aaron Burr.

Burr had run for president against Thomas Jefferson. He lost. Jefferson became the third president of the United States in 1801. Burr felt Hamilton had helped Jefferson win. He also said Hamilton had insulted him. He challenged Hamilton to a **duel**. The two men fired pistols at each other. Burr killed Hamilton with one shot.

Hamilton was only 49 years old when he was killed.

Alexander Hamilton played a very important role in the formation of the U.S.A. He was never president. But he will always be remembered as one of America's greatest leaders.

Timeline of Alexander Hamilton's Life

1755 > **1773** > **1777** >

Born on January 11

Moves to New York City

Becomes aide to General George Washington

Named first
secretary of
the Treasury
⋮

Killed in duel
with Aaron Burr
⋮

1780 > **1789** > **1795** > **1804**

Marries Elizabeth
Schuyler

Goes back
to being a
lawyer

A Poem About Alexander Hamilton

He was born on an island, very poor—
and Alexander wanted more.
He came to America, worked hard and long
to make our country free and strong.

You Can Be a Leader

Find something you feel strongly about and learn all you can about it.

Share your views with others.

Do not be afraid to run for office in a school election—or to support someone else you believe in.

Glossary

- **colony** (KAH-luh-nee): territory that has been settled by people from another country and is controlled by that country

- **determined** (dih-TUR-mind): having or showing a strong intention to do something

- **duel** (DOO-uhl): fight between two people using swords or guns, fought according to strict rules

- **Treasury** (TREZH-uh-ree): government department that is in charge of collecting taxes and managing public money

Index

Facts for Now

Visit this Scholastic Web site for more information on
Alexander Hamilton and download the Teaching Guide for this series:

www.factsfornow.scholastic.com

Enter the keywords Alexander Hamilton

About the Author

K.C. Kelley has written dozens of biographies for young readers,
including books on the Wright brothers, Betsy Ross, Jesse Owens, and
Milton Hershey. K.C. once lived in New Jersey, where Hamilton fought in the
Revolutionary War.